errata

Crab Orchard Series in Poetry
Open Competition Award

errata

poems by

LISA FAY COUTLEY

Crab Orchard Review &
Southern Illinois University Press
Carbondale

18 17 16 15   4 3 2 1

The Crab Orchard Series in Poetry is a joint publishing venture of Southern
Illinois University Press and *Crab Orchard Review*. This series has been
made possible by the generous support of the Office of the President of
Southern Illinois University and the Office of the Vice Chancellor for
Academic Affairs and Provost at Southern Illinois University Carbondale.

Editor of the Crab Orchard Series in Poetry: Jon Tribble
Judge for the 2014 Open Competition Award: Adrienne Su

Cover illustration: partially deconstructed clay model for bronze sculpture,
    Self Betrayal, by Eric Michael Wilson, © 2014 (www.ericwilsonart.com).
Cover design adapted by Kelly Brooks from an original design by Erin
    Kirk New.

Library of Congress Cataloging-in-Publication Data
Coutley, Lisa Fay.
[Poems. Selections]
Errata / Lisa Fay Coutley.
    pages ; cm. — (Crab Orchard Series in Poetry)
Summary: "A finely wrought poetry collection about love, loss, and the will
    to continue in the face of adversity and struggle"— Provided by publisher.
ISBN 978-0-8093-3448-3 (softcover : acid-free paper) —
    ISBN 0-8093-3448-8 (softcover : acid-free paper) —
    ISBN 978-0-8093-3449-0 (ebook)
I. Title.
PS3603.O88823A6 2015
811'.6—dc23   2015016769

Printed on recycled paper. ♻

The paper used in this publication meets the minimum requirements of
    American National Standard for Information Sciences—Permanence of
    Paper for Printed Library Materials, ANSI Z39.48-1992. ∞

For Fay-Fay

I am no more your mother
Than the cloud that distils a mirror to reflect its own slow
Effacement at the wind's hand.

—Sylvia Plath

Contents

Acknowledgments

Many thanks to the editors of the following publications where these poems first appeared, sometimes in different versions:

American Literary Review: "Shooting Geese,"

American Poetry Journal: "My Desert"

Barn Owl Review: "For My First Dog"

Blackbird: "During the Final Scene" and "Why to Bury a Parrot"

Boxcar Poetry Review: "Elegy for a Skinwalker"

Cave Wall: "My Lake" and "View from the High Road"

Clackamas Literary Review: "Driving Drunk, & a Dozen White Crosses"

Connotation Press: "The Way the Plot"

Country Dog Review: "Love & Squall"

Cream City Review: "Driving Up-Canyon with My Two Teen Sons" and "Self Portrait as Pyrocumulonimbus"

DMQ Review: "Coffee"

Drunken Boat: "Ode to Postpartum"

Eclipse: "Dirty Fruit"

Failbetter: "Self-Portrait as Mountains Surrounding a Dry Lakebed"

Fugue: "Woman from Water"

Harpur Palate: "Chicken Soup"

Hayden's Ferry Review: "Barefoot on the Pulpit"

Hollins Critic: "On Home"

Iron Horse Literary Review: "Family Portrait as the Language of Disaster" and "Small Break in the Cirrocumulus"

Juked: "The Lapidary Speaks"

Kenyon Review Online: "Researchers Find Mice Pass On Trauma to Subsequent Generations"

Linebreak: "Errata"

Ninth Letter: "Careo"

Pedestal Magazine: "Posing for Aunt Sandy"

Poet Lore: "Ode to the Bottle"

RHINO: "Listen"

Seneca Review: "Dear Morpheus—"

Sou'wester: "When He Comes at Me"

Tar Wolf Review: "Commute"

Third Coast: "Patientia"

32 Poems: "Respiration"

Weave: "Sadly, There Was No Dog Bite"

"My Lake" was reprinted in *Best New Poets 2010*, guest edited by Claudia Emerson.

"View from the High Road," "Barefoot on the Pulpit," and "To Sleep" were reprinted on *Verse Daily*.

"Barefoot on the Pulpit" was reprinted in *The Best of Kore Press 2012*, published by Kore Press, and named a *Verse Daily* Favorite Poem of 2011.

"Her Father Says She Worries Too Much" was reprinted in *Two Weeks*, an e-anthology published by *Linebreak*.

"Careo" was reprinted in the *2013 Best of the Net Anthology*, guest edited by A. E. Stallings.

Heartfelt thanks as well to the editors at Black Lawrence Press and Articles Press for publishing some of these poems in the chapbooks *In the Carnival of Breathing* (2011) and *Back-Talk* (2010).

This book would not exist without the guidance and generous support I've received from professors, students, and staff at the University of Wisconsin–Green Bay, Northern Michigan University, the University of Utah, the Sewanee Writers' Conference, and the Bread Loaf Writers' Conference. Rebecca Meacham, Aeron Haynie, Austin Hummell, Beverly Matherne, Leslie Adrienne Miller, John Rybicki, Erin O'Connell, Jacqueline Osherow, and

Katharine Coles—I am forever grateful for your encouragement and mentorship.

So many keen readers and buoying friends have influenced the currents of this book, but I would like to give special thanks to Traci Brimhall, Sandra Beasley, Eric Smith, Kimberly Johnson, Lillian-Yvonne Bertram, Laura Eve Engel, and Michelle Chan Brown. Also, sincere thanks to Eric Wilson and Kelly Brooks for their keen artistic visions and contributions to the cover design.

My immense gratitude to the National Endowment for the Arts Literature Fellowships program, for awarding me a fellowship in 2013, during which time I was able to see this book through to its final version. And to Adrienne Su, Jon Tribble, the Crab Orchard Series in Poetry staff, and the Southern Illinois University Press staff, thank you so much for bringing this book to life.

Finally, to Linda, for always answering the phone; to Cody and Channer, for following me everywhere these poems have taken us; to Tina, for believing in me; to my dad, for instilling in me a need for music; and to my mom, for helping me to see that I must keep dancing even after the music stops—all of my love.

one

Shooting Geese,

I'll maintain, is a thing I did for love.
　　　　At fifteen, a girl will crouch in the blind
　　　　　　until her toes go numb, eager

to prove her aim. It's hard to know how far she'll go
　　　　over slick rocks at the shore's edge
　　　　　　lugging her body weight in decoys

for a boy. A boy who'll later trace with his finger
　　　　the white smudge growing inside her, nothing
　　　　　　more than a sonogram, & ask if it is

too late. Changing my mind at the right time
　　　　has never been my strength. I'd wait.
　　　　　　I'd hold my breath with the water

as my witness, my finger loose against the trigger,
　　　　taking direction not from that north wind
　　　　　　or whitecaps or silhouettes circling

plastic geese, so when that boy mouthed *now*
　　　　through clenched teeth it never occurred to me
　　　　　　that I might have been their first

warning, might have pointed toward the sun
　　　　rising & fired both rounds, as if to say no,
　　　　　　I won't bait them, won't

watch them glide toward those empty shells
　　　　so much like themselves, but I let them fall
　　　　　　one by one to the dark of that water.

By their necks, like bouquets, I held them up
           as proof, then lay them in a row on shore.
                      There, on my knees, I gripped them

each in turn & spun their bodies counterclockwise
           against the stillness of their heads,
                just in case, just to be sure.

Elegy for a Skinwalker

When he says October, he needs me to praise leaves
taking apart their light, months spent feeding to fast
because the man I love moved to the desert & fell
for a plastic bag, a hip of wind snagged on a spiral
of barbwire. Anything Orwellian, any ashy tongue
steeped in suffering turns him on. Still, he wants
his dog's breath hanging over this lake's edge, my
hand so cold there's a reason to clutch away fight.

So Love I say, today the water is just below calm,
all ribs not breaking but nicked. Here's rust & plum,
bruise & orange. Here is a dying we can all embrace.
Bring dormancy, colorless sleep. Today at the beach
I threw a stick for a dog that wasn't there. Her face?
I can't remember. I'll believe in green when I see it.

Ode to the Bottle

Vessel of every desperate letter lost
between one time zone & another, sun-
starched but never wet, we forgive you.

What you lack in transit, you make up
in bust & tumble, in your cobalt blue.
In fact, we thank you. For letting Brad

kiss Jenny in the basement, for showing
the hand a shape it knew in the dark.
You, bottle, who housed the lightning

bugs & grasshoppers & our earliest surges
of spark, from leather to the ends of our hair.
Branded, reused, & broken, you are

a weapon in reverse, a symphony of anger
tossed from a moving car, the most popular
little spoon on the street. For always staying

in the bag, for always being there, here's to
you, bottle, to that sailboat you carry inside:
always full of wind, always going nowhere.

Driving Drunk, & a Dozen White Crosses

from her purse to her palm, she revs her cemetery
        toward a gauzy daymoon, curves our Buick

the hipbend home. Mouthfuls of ditch flowers
        purple & passing, cottonwoods spilling

that moon's confetti, the coal in Mother's eyes
        whitening. This is the fire I warm my hands by.

Clear the deadwood & you'll see: nothing but a girl
        with a mouth dry of music. Let's pretend

this is thirst, when a girl might stagger three, maybe four
        days before paving her own mirage: a single drop

of oil down a harp string. Rain. Under this influence,
        it will take years to learn she's a room she drags

with her. Wall-to-wall nettles she's shaped into banjos,
        maracas, a flute. When it finally comes time to sit

at the river, she'll have to finger her throat, snap in halves
        all the notes that woman sung into her—

granite specks from hammer to chisel to headstone—
        until the horse in her heart stamps its hooves again.

Researchers Find Mice Pass On Trauma to
Subsequent Generations

Even before I was born, before my father
        took my mother's head in his hands,
                her black curls like sprockets

sprung from his palms, & held her face
        under the lukewarm water of our tub,
                her belly a heavy globe—my only

armor—pressed against that bright white
        porcelain, before I took my first breath
                two months after my father failed

to cinch it, her, I mastered a palpable fear
        of choking. It's all a mind game, Dad
                would say, shoving another M&M

in my mouth: swallow. Pseudodysphagia—
        even before I learned the word I knew
                the shame that came from fearing

fear rooted in the fiction of my mind—hers
                & hers & hers & hers.

Dear Morpheus—

Stop bringing her to this silent cinema
where I'm forever disappointed   waiting

for the dead to speak. Instead
of a voice, you make mute gestures

through a woman so young & healthy
I weep. I mourn her with my face

buried in the crook of her white sleeve
because down the hall she eats paint

from my bedroom wall. Fleck by fleck,
drops them on her tongue & washes them

with whiskcy.   Oh, Morpheus—

Let this be the sacrament of my small body:
the girl who had to be carried from the bus,

refusing to pledge allegiance without her mom.
Let this be the moment she doesn't leave me

waiting, but the moment she takes me home
to the lovely body I thought was mine

to save. Give her back. Throw her over
this need. Let her be my breakwall. My firewall.

Recite the prayer of the white sweater
all night   down my dark & narrow dream.

Posing for Aunt Sandy

I am twelve in the mirror
of my mother's oak dresser
when that radio chokes
out a slow country song
& the room is a lens closing
around us. Hold them, she says,
turns my two palms over
& I pose with a gel breast
in one, wig in the other.

The shine of my June hair falls
straight to my navel, past two
crescent moons tangled in tree.
Aunt Sandy's head is all the night,
all the heat of our last summer
drive when she'll die rough
as a car. That Montana sun,
that shoulderless road. A radiator
heaving with one dusty lung.

When death rattles its infant
born to die in my aunt's liver,
it tears all the wet paper
of my mother's mind.
She will never be more
than a front-row chair.
I turn my hands from the blue
music of rain to cup
one breast, one artifact.

Emptying the Red Vase

At home, a woman doesn't have to face herself,
doesn't have to pretend to favor the sweet

side of a drink. She wants her whiskey straight
at the kitchen table. Wants no one to see her

fall, no one to lift her from linoleum.
There's no one worth smiling for anyway.

Not since the curtains went up & she stayed
to breathe in the whole kitchen.

The doors of a security ward shut,
& she struggles with the blunt edges

of a ten-piece puzzle. A circle of men
look right through her. They're looking

to me. They're passing the burning bottle.

Why to Bury a Parrot

When I slow for the fox crossing Grove Street
outside the house the Jehovahs hole up in,
I nearly follow its wounds—
the white of its tail dimming a light
through water, through wood.

I ease off the brake, roll Grove's hill
to the stoplight & turn toward those cliffs
where I dropped my bird in a jewelry box,
still singing. It was winter then, ice tilting,
ice swaying like buoys between black rock.

Never was a winged thing so willing to be caged.
When the sky was a circling hawk, a human hand
brighter than sun. Escape as foreign as the perch
of a tree. This morning, fog closing down
around the cove where the birdsong stopped,

I consider my own cargo bay doors,
the ship in each of us sinking. The breath-held
moments when that box just hung there
knocking its wood against ice. I would dive
through water so cold the dead never rise,

water foxhole dark, & try to stay under,
to follow that silver latch rusting at rock bottom.
I would unclasp its hymns, all those blinding notes,
but this woman's body, this broken clay jar
is not meant to level such pressure.

The Way the Plot

always unexpectedly the apple
   falls rotten from the top
      tier of the wire basket

dull thud dumb roll always
   while your back is turned
      & you're spooling

noodles with the small clean fork
   on any otherwise quiet day
      so it strikes you like a man

you loved silhouetted against a garage
   wall behind your bright headlights
      holding the cordless phone

away from his face that tells you everything
   the chaplain on the other end will say
      about slight snow just covering

pine needles & maple leaves   soft soft webbing
   beneath that cracked bathroom window
      where your mother did not fall

soaping in the shower or suffer a stroke
   folding laundry or prepare you
      for loss that nails your knees

to this filthy floor   that forever catch-
   of-breath when wrist-deep in warm
      water hips pressed just enough

against the sink to forget a moment
        of your weight hips just past craving
                his hands to your sway some

fruit you meant to eat hums low
        in the throat of every paradise
                you've been asked to leave.

Respiration

& so it begins, with a slap on the ass,
an open mouth, & something foreign.
We say air where once there was water,
but that isn't right. Pretend you've been
asleep at sea with a navy in your chest,
in your *Unterseeboot*. To wake is to begin
them moving your cargo through hostile
waters with a promise of never leaving
the vessel, of maintaining radio silence,
& with a perfect naval crew you neither
fall nor float. Your officers shift their hats
& deal gin rummy in a teardrop hull
that never crackles, in a shallow seabed
where they never strike a rudder or time
the missiles. They are geared up but never
engaged in combat, & they seem happy
enough. Until one day. Say someone loses
the king of spades or steals a porno mag
from a bunkmate. It's been too long
with no word from home, waiting for a war
that never comes. It ends then, with a fist
in the face, dogpiled men caught
in a promise to neither leave nor love
one another, a fire lit in an airtight vessel
where no one can open the door.

two

On Home

All winter long my sons have pointed guns
in my face & with their mouths popped

the triggers. The oldest wants to spoon me.
The youngest wants to change his name

to *the playground pimp*. When we circle up
for dinner, I'm careful not to say chicken *breast*

or meat*ball* or anything they can follow with
that's what she said. Consider the going rate

for hormones, then picture an eager group
of eBay bidders. I joke, but someone should

tell these boys—in a wake of black mascara,
mothers drive away. All winter long I've left

feel-good Post-its on the bathroom mirror,
the espresso maker, the edge of my razor.

Every day I've given myself reasons to stay.

Coffee

What's strange is that I never stopped
opening my eyes in that room without
windows, that *tomb* we said & agreed
standing was better than lying down—
even when you called me girl I didn't
stop to reach for names. You shawled
our bodies with bedsheets & claimed
some alien sense from a nub at the base
of your head. You found my tongue there
every morning. Mine was the loneliness
of waking, a woman with common knots.
Outside, the leashes taut, the tugged men,
the rain flaying long-strided strangers
in ordinary clothes. A prism in a kitchen
window, day-old coffee grounds, cigarette
filters spinning in a toilet bowl. Puddles
never spoke to me. We were something
I could climb, root by root & naked
while another woman's hair still mapped
your pillow. If I believed in signs, this
was the urgency of homing bones. Sweat
real as a candle pushed back on its nail.
Those mornings we sipped coffee blacker
than I could stand, I never said bitter—
even when you started using my name
in bed. No one wants to be simple
as blame or the word *anger*, so I held
my tongue to something foreign.
I never asked for anything sweet.

Dirty Fruit

I see my son's bare butt & imagine
my father: seven, whimpering against the groan
of a heavy door, a nurse with a cigarette.

He is tired of living
already. Beyond this summer,
typhoid fever, this hospital bed,

he will barb like wire
& shove love down basement steps.
A war, a marriage, three grandkids

later, he dips his fingers in the shit
& piss closet of quarantine & holds
my nose to his final sickroom.

Eggshell walls, figure eights in plaster,
matches & Black Cats Uncle Eddy sneaks
through a slit in his screen, the *Giant*

Jungle Coloring Book Grandma leaves
at his door. Between two pages
of uncolored lions, deep in the open spine

of a rabid world, he cleaves fireworks
like pickets, curses the unwashed fruit,
& strikes a match

to the smell of everyone risking
love enough to die for my father.

Listen

Lately, my father's body is telling him
no. No sleep. No ladders. No tilling
the winter from a square of dirt. Betrayal

is the blindness of tomatoes, he says, in a world
full of rabbits & squirrels. A man can hardly catch
his breath. Even the dentist is muttering prayers

for the last tooth in his gums, though my father's
certain there's no good reason for such a thing
to be saved. Open a mouth & pull. Done.

He's never believed in lifelong love—that
there's nowhere you can go but backward
when you dream. Lately, he simply hopes

he's man enough to watch my children play
at the beach, to hear them laugh & not feel
jealous. I could say it's true—that drowning

doesn't look like drowning, that euphoria begins
as a person nears death, that hunger & thirst
will no longer exist—but my father's spent

his whole life telling me to shut up & listen.
I won't tell him that hearing is the last sense
to go. That I believe. I'll never stop talking.

During the Final Scene

Even then, in those early days,
time was a lukewarm bathtub.
You steadied your wrist & pooled
a Palindrome Fossil with a floating hand
to circumnavigate the dial, my smiling
sun & moon clock, the wall clocks,
alarm clocks, even our tiny hour-
glass timer from the top of the stove—
put them all in a silver bucket,
buttoned your jeans, pulled on your boots
& marched them to the backyard
where you buried them in a dream
during the final scene of *Apocalypse Now.*
All this time spent to say it was nothing,
really. Yet we both knew the value
of two beers & a shared cigarette.
What happened? That was the question
when you opened your eyes to my side
of the couch, but you'd been so late
in waking, so long in gathering, so diligent
stockpiling all our time, I said *nothing*
& we held there, watching the credits.

Her Father Says She Worries Too Much

but she's only trying to prepare
        for the worst in a world of paper
            lamps & Zippo lighters,

at a breakfast nook with two teen sons
        whose yolks *explode* in their mouths
            & *drip* on their plates—

one who cuts his meat into man-sized
        bites with a butter knife & gags
            at every meal, & another

who eyes how she chews & maneuvers
        a city of four-way stops, where no one
            bothers with turn signals—

so it's only right to worry: to bite & tear,
        to pluck & push & touch again,
            again, to vex with her teeth

& shoulder the paper-lamp light
        alone; because today a man passed
            as she perched on black

rock, watching him skim the water
        in a Coast Guard boat—the kind
            designed to absorb spiller

waves & still remain sturdy—the man
        who could be her life, who sees her
            through binoculars,

who would turn starboard & stop
    if he weren't rushing to save someone
        else, while she's there, flailing

in her mind, where the cat has knocked
    a pan from the propane stove, in her
        home that she's certain is burning.

Chicken Soup

It's likely you're right that no one's watching
in my window while I'm mincing the garlic
& thinking of how I wasn't holding a knife
but standing in the health center trying not to
touch the chairs or the square pillar in the middle
of the room, trying harder to hold my jaw closed
as a helicopter laid flat the grass in North Carolina
where they found the body of that small, small girl
with the curly hair & the smile. She smiles still
as I switch to chopping onion & stop crying
over mothers who sell daughters for sex, so now
I'm crying because I never fall in love with men
who love me first, & because every time I call
the doctor my earache & sore throat go away,
& the chill of the stethoscope, the stranger's tug
at the front of my shirt, the feeling that someone's
looking in where I can't see out—that's gone, too,
& no one should go on faking their cough alone.

After the Fire
    for Channer

I'm tucking amulets between the bandages
because my son hears his dead dog
breathing, & he won't touch imaginary things.

Like sharp-force trauma has its story to tell
of the axe, char has its story to tell of the fire,
but the lazy Braille of burnt bone disguises

our size, so *how will we find each other in heaven?*
I can never explain. Instead, I sing a song
about wonder & stars to put him to sleep

though I don't believe in magic. He knows
the bony landmarks, the latticework of clay,
that it takes an artist to reconstruct a face.

No matter. He staples his sketches
to telephone poles. At busy intersections,
he clutches his jar of pennies. The phone

call we miss every day is probably God,
who refuses to leave a voicemail, to take
a small reward. My son is searching for air

underwater, for stars on the soles of his feet,
for the bird that will eat from his open palm.

Sadly, There Was No Dog Bite

When I pulled that gun, just to get you
to let me through the door, I could see
(over your shoulder, into the yard)
snow, falling round as horses' eyes
in June.
        The trees were old bones,
bending because it was asked of them.
Our voices broke like water & plumed
against a breakwall in my head. We froze
midbreath.
        When I pulled that gun
from a drawer, just to get by, I should have
lassoed my love, reigned in my combat-
boot girl & taken your last cigarette
for the drive,
        should have seen how snow
falls hard as human hearts & trees moan
weak ballads for summer's wind. A trigger
is a finger, mapping out the stillness
of futures apart
        when it's together we see.
We were full of last chances & second
guesses, strangers sharing a strip of carpet,
rubbing every raw knot of our backs
to erase the stench
        of longing.
We were going to prove the singularity
of a snowflake. Take this forest, these trees
& bring night to its knees again. Yet when
I pulled that gun,

not a god could be seen
through our window. Sadly, there was no dog
bite, no rabid grief to throw over the day, just
the sort of end at such an end when snow falls
in June, & leaves shuck summer from their skin.

Goodbye in the Voice of My Father

I tell you what: tornadoes are the most violent
mothers, big rigs plowing through wall clouds
with hail hammering hard as rocks. They move

southwest to northeast, so you're heading right
for them. You know, a twister can lift a motel
sign from the ground in Oklahoma & dump it

in Arkansas, just like a bird from the deep south
was carried three states north once & found itself
all alone. Lost. A *normal* bird'll nest near the nest

where it was born.
                        He leans my car door shut
& doesn't hug me, just warns me of the way I am
moving across the country, a bird slung by storm

or the storm itself. A vacancy sign. He hates me
for leaving. Himself, for shoving me from the nest.

Self-Portrait as Pyrocumulonimbus

Don't ask me why men want from this
    peculiar pulse, skipping cul-de-sacs
        & riverbeds. I eat like a woman

        ravenous until the forest is a field
    standing black with javelins. I catapult
into clear sky. Because God loosed me

from that better wound, braiding anger
    up my spine & between ground & cloud
        bellowed the flame, they crave.

        They say *destruction* as if they don't
    want to follow. Don't study how I hover
above them, cracking my ribs apart,

peeling lightning from my thighs. They pray
    for my unruly heart, may it be their weapon.
        They misunderstand. My desire

        is air, threading vengeance
    into the dress I'd wear if I woke
each morning in a bed half slept in,

but I don't sleep. I wander. I err. I lunge
    into ductwork & become the bedroom,
        the porch swing, the yellow grass

        around the concrete deer. I keep
    hoping for a day when burn won't breed
ash, & we can return home, devoured

by hunger neither mine nor theirs, but fear
        unleashed refuses the chain. The fruit
                is my miracle is my palm is my water

                effacing the blaze. I would surrender
        my mouth to rain if they didn't beg from me
the bite-bruise on both shoulders *again, again.*

Woman from Water

I went west from water to learn drier states,
climb steeper grades & test those runaway
truck routes—all uphill, all gravel. Alone

was the way to what meant desert. There I was
digging in firebeds & rigging steel traps
beneath day-old coals, letting the mouth remain

open & silent. Be it bobcat or coyote I caught
so long as my eyes glowed in its eyes, wild.
Once, far clouds stilled to notice me floating

between sun & stone. Woman from water.
But once is a way to say something's been
lost. If every yesterday has a man in it, what

can I see in all this rock? Here are the steeples,
there are the thrones, nothing but girl-shaped
pillars, still as mortared doors. I cannot open

to the time before a house was carved down
around me, before I was an altar to a single grain
of sand. Who could help but look back? I didn't

know how to say that I wanted to be seen
heading west—a woman setting traps & still
starving. Hunger as a time I've misunderstood.

I am guilty of baiting mirage & leaving water,
for pretending what's reflected by wave is
distorted, as if I've ever really wanted to look.

three

My Lake

My lake has many rooms & one, which is red
with a door that's always open but chained.
My lake owns boxing gloves. She owns lingerie.
She can swing, she can cha-cha, she can salsa
& tap but refuses a simple slow dance. My lake
learned early to rest the needle without a scratch.
She has been classically trained in lovemaking.
When she wants to ride a rollercoaster, she does
it alone. When she lets her hair down, men go
blind. My lake doesn't take any shit. She wears
stilettos in ice storms, does crosswords in pen.
She eats red meat. Her porch needs painting,
her flowers need weeding, but my lake reads
palms in twelve different languages. If my lake
puts her hand to your chest, she decides. At times,
whole days can pass when she won't let anyone
near her. She freezes just before she murders
her own shore. It's been years, & still my lake
won't name the delicate sound of ice taking
then brushing away. She might say it's the train
of a wedding dress, or the rain falling on a glass
slipper. There are times she sees the grace of two
loons gliding—their bodies a duet over breaking
water, & she slows herself. She makes a cradle.

In Which Dorothy Appears

In a meadow of poppies, we sleep before the snow
falls & wakes all but you. No cheekbones to trace,

no crystal ball when you go. No one who hears
the branches that scratch this daughter's window.

Red tree. Dark morning. Gut-punch of gone.
Sometimes it takes just one gust of wind to forget

a mother's face. Twice Dorothy woke in worlds
she didn't know, & twice she met the same friends

in a different place. I need someone to explain.
Show me a road & I'll follow, follow, follow . . .

What is a black box if it holds nothing but bone?
This beach sand & gravel, ashes for answers.

Of all those fall nights that we sat to the Zenith,
no one saw Dorothy's mom. We got Emily

& Henry. A terrier. Some witches. A twister.
If this is about remembering, it's about believing.

Let a window frame slap my face.
Let me forget some other story.

Driving Up-Canyon with My Two Teen Sons

or Boys I & II as I've come to call them (or swear
     at them) this year, laying the fencework of broken
        bottles all around me, even now, as we push

faster up a blinding canyon road. Look, boys, here
     even crag reaches straight for the sun (& I can't
        help but tell them we each want to burn);

look at how the aspens stand together from one
     long root, but they'll never touch each other
        above ground; look at the single spruce

that grew back-against-a-cliff-wall, facing only road
     (as I'm speeding up a lane that snakes to nowhere
        I can see). This, you'll never understand.

Like the way I arrange sunflowers on the coffee table
     in our new home. Have you noticed how they reach
        for sun or soil, where there's only ceiling,

only vase. This, kids, is the year we'll write our history
     of black ice & snow. Here, each of you hold
        a wiper blade, & I'll accelerate, eyes closed.

Commute

It happens when I'm driving.
I see a woman at a bus stop,

gray & frail, frump-
backed in a tattered coat,

looking older than she should.
In the space of a shallow breath,

I'm certain she's you—
pinning shame, chin to chest,

tugging an outgrowth of witchy bangs,
one hand fisted, tucked against tweed.

I know that woman cannot be you. Still,
some mornings, I slip my feelings

into the pockets of a stranger
& send them off on a bus.

In the Carnival of Breathing

Call it a burning building or a sinking ship,
either way you're in it when you phone to say
you can't tie your shoelaces. I say report card,

a boy who rips the sole from his shoe on purpose,
alveoli. Not sure what this has to do with plants,
you say—this burning ship, this sinking building.

I'm not either. On tossing nights, I get out of bed
to smoke, just to watch my breath in, to see it out.
I tied my first laces on old clown shoes, one bunny

ear over another, under, through & pulled tight,
easy as a cursive L or anything else before Velcro.
Here's a burning building. There's a sinking ship.

Here's me, two arms bent for buckets. There's you,
two faces shaking through water, through smoke.
I'm double-knotting the world's shoelaces for you

but the carousel keeps spinning, the balloons
keep twisting themselves into silent llama-dogs.
Maybe we're all barking buildings, spitting ships,
all the laces in a sailor's knot, a fistful of spoons.

Twelve Days Scrubbing the Dead

Twelve days I've knelt at your brittle helices
        & cold toes, your trigger finger

on a can of peaches, angel at the foot of your bed.
        What is it that turns to vinegar

between a woman & her girl?
        I have been angrier than ice.

The whole bruise of night pulled down
        around you, & you stretched

your pale thighs—two tapering lines
        where I signed my name. I'm tired

of driving this shoulderless road, charred
        bone through a desert tunnelway.

I'm trying to riddle you home like salt
        leeched through a sheet of red rock.

Juniper's last cracked root, the mind twists
        for water. Even the ravens won't cry

when to leave. The succulents all cloaked
        in chicken wire. Oh, Mother. You

chinful of hairs. You husk. Maybe you were right.
        I should have slept with my bra on.

Careo

Which means I've started watching YouTube
clips from the local dog shelter in the city
I was sure I'd burned behind us. Familiar
never pushes in its chair or leaves the table

quiet. We live in a box. At night, I lock us
inside & hope no one breaks in, or out.
Sometimes, presleep, I spin scenarios
of what might happen. My sons never make it

to college or marriage or fatherhood.
I try to imagine how my whole life has passed
& only this year have I noticed my own

pigeon-toed stride. Parked, I'm stalking
my oldest boy as he walks from school
to his friend's, where they'll sit, *chillin'*
& smokin' blunts all day. & so love saunters

dumbly away. No glancing back. This is it:
the dream where I'm screaming underwater
or trying to punch some bitch in the face.
Voiceless. Armless. *Careo—in need of, free*

from, without. A kenneled dog comes closer
to the word for missing than this dead language
I'm learning, in this house where no one speaks.

Self-Portrait as Mountains Surrounding a Dry Lakebed

Forget that no one asks to be here, fault & collision.
      Forget that I seem incapable of suffering, am
            liable to break. The word fragile, the word

impassable, forget words simple, stranded as bones
      I cannot swallow. Begging & tenor, the mono-
            chrome Flats as tender ice Earth seems to be

curving away. What isn't snow is salt. What isn't
      light is blinding. What isn't language is flesh
            cut of the moon slowly rolling. A dying

lake can never recite every night every name
      every star a blade dulled against another
            ox's rib cage. Let there be no cairn

to the jagged trail of wagons. No line no child
      draws in the sand. No, picture lonely more
            precise. I have seen the smallest ones

urged first with gaunt & watering cheeks
      to the bodies of the dead, crying *forgive me*
            father, as mother turns away to chew

his last shoelace. The fire will roar but I cannot
      stop the freeze, her turn, the sleep she'll sleep
            without feeling both feet burn.

Char that I never sorry to say, I plead. Winds
      from such a height they never end. Winds
            from such a height I never asked.

Ash over Utah

That day in June, too
close to the day spent

blinking bone from my eyes,
where desert willows flip

their hair like silver coins
& hummingbirds work the wombs

of thistle & primrose. In the Valley
of the Gods, we are without

a want for chaos, for jutting steeples.
Here, between red ridges of wind-

worn sandstone, in the remains
of a parched landscape, I watch

rock wanting to part—
a chicken balanced on an egg,

you in a black plastic box. I bury
what's left, stall, then toss you

to this wind that breathes
a fire of flowers out.

The Lapidary Speaks

It's the greatest thing—
        when you realize there is no death.

That it all takes place at a dinner table
    without linens or forks or neckties
        & we ask for refills of wine

without recognizing that every time
    we dive in the ocean, we're only going
        for a swim. To cut a cabochon

or trace an agate is to know these ruins
    will never go quiet. Have you noticed
        how sky holds the water down—

a woman's palms over a pleated skirt?
    She says inured, she says noise churned,
        she says swallow & moon

your own tide. Tonight: brush your teeth,
    then eat. At some point, the chassis
        will rattle & you'll come home

as expected as a bedroom closet.
    The table never changes
        the chairs, always mellifluous

rips in a current toward open sea, where
    the wind's fetch is without limitation
        & everything tumbled thrums.

Patientia

Of which I have none & much, so I want you
       to stumble in, kick off your boots, light
              a cigarette in the living room, just

so I can tell you to go back out again. Patience.
       Suffering. Endurance. I have much & none
              & have yet to learn the word

for *missing*. I say *you*, but there is no *you*. There is
       only a girl, balancing the weight of a hand-
              gun large as her forearm, taking aim

at an egg in a haystack. Only the small smoke
       after the shot that I play back again
              & again but never see

the egg, breaking. Only fragments of shell.
       The moment of connect is the moment
              of disconnect I've been

on my knees for—needling through hay—
       not for the transformation but the record
              of which hand you used

to pull the door when you left. There is only a photo,
       now, of your dog near a shoreline, her face
              turned to the west, the sun

setting pink in her mouth. Only a girl, breathing
       through the kickback—her legs spread,
              her shot straight. She & I:

whispering to an outline of a shadow. Because bodies,
we know, are built for falling. The last leaves
rustle, & from across the street,

lying in the arm of a tree, I know this is a new place.
I don't know what I'm aiming for anymore,
but I know she still likes to aim.

four

Errata

As the story goes, the raven's wings
aren't black. They're waves capping
dark omens. Crows with curtained throats.
Who knows what falls from the shelf
inside us. Even gods skin their knees
to bleed. The man at the end of the aisle
is pocketing two-for-one toothbrushes.
The cashier is hand-perking her breasts
& picking her teeth with a receipt.
I'm sorry you won't see your son, his skin
peeling its white scarf through blizzards.
I haven't sanded the road, won't
strut across town in my ballet slippers.
Your shape in this bed is my shape.
Erase my whole notes from your page.
Two stoplights ago, the wind
off a pickup pulled us further from home.
When I said the moonlight made graves
to square off the night, I meant to say
pull over. Listen: my heart's a gutter
of ravens tugging at the firmament.

Family Portrait as the Language of Disaster

Each day this year, one of us has declared
some state of emergency: a broken wrist,
a faulty video game, an unwashed dish.

As governor, translating such acts of god
has meant scouting disaster—both natural
& domestic—as hazard, so it's no surprise

when my lover complains I'm entrenched
in the preempt of ruin, securing the perimeter
with broken bottles along every wall. What

he means to say is I've imposed curfews,
controlled access to my disaster site, ordered
evacuations. It's his place or no place, & any-

way, his face doesn't fit this portrait. So what
if I'm testing every fragile object in my home
against the curb. I'm preparing my sons

for the relics of life. The aftermath, I know,
takes voice even in the quiet determination
of an endless walk after all the trains halt.

Ours won't be an earthquake or a hurricane,
a hailstorm followed by a tornado. I've claimed
our state's only criminal incident will be arson.

I've taken it upon myself to commandeer
a chicken leg, a peanut butter jar, & deodorant
in order to diagram One Response to Anger

against the dining room wall. I'll be the match.
You, boys, be the binding threads created
by disaster. There's no other state to call for help.

Love & Squall

Ask me to choose between rough
water & a stone path leading nowhere
I can see, & I'll focus on the yellow
raincoat hung from a row of hooks.
The wall, the whitecaps, the dark hill
shown through two separate windows
can never meet. So I need to pretend
that beyond what can be seen, a single
clothesline is thrashing its frayed end
against a weathered pole. Neglect. Time.
I need to believe in what was left behind.
To see the yellow is to miss the door
left open—the urgency of what was
washed to sea, of what crested a hill.
As if the world we believed were still
as canvas, nothing but edges. As if what
was here we'll always know as abandon, hips
once battened to a gritty floor. The tremor
of shadows our candles cast during a storm.
The empty latch hole in the doorframe
says longing. The binoculars hung over
the yellow slicker beg wait—I'm still
waiting. Don't ask me to choose one
of two starfish propped against a pane
in the only sunlight streaking through
this small piece of room, where one
of two lovers stands watch. Mine are two
hands, reaching during a squall, brittle

enough to grasp at anything unseen
through this window, over this dark hill,
obstructed by this wall. I'll hold anything
that promises to be so violent, so brief.

When He Comes at Me

the first time, I'm still trying to decide
    over-easy, scrambled, or poached,
        yet already I'm bracing

the egg in the bed of my palm. Instinct
    is a sea turtle lumbering toward open
        ocean, a honeybee dancing

the knowledge of pollen, a newborn
    rooting & suckling. I'm imagining
        a dog with its tail straight

& its hackles raised the second time
    his jaw locks & his eyes go black
        with fight. Love is the absence

of menace, the urge to keep the fire
    churned, the lock secure in its latch.
        To move the stars around

the sky, close one eye, say something is
    different. My son, you are not yet
        a man, so when you come

at me a third time, I'm still trying to
    decide which of us has grown
        meaner. My hands are

shadows in front of my face, shapes
    of anger you see when you look
        in the mirror. Mother

is not a word either of us has
      rehearsed. This is the world
            I dare down into sleep

each night, in a bed I force myself into
      with myself. Dressing in the dark,
            we are fumbling with the lock.

Ode to Postpartum

Or to the girl who ate fruit with abandon.
Plum juice & peach pit, the necessary mess
& the fist of labor. To bear down one's teeth

into bone & skin of all things living & live
for more than the girl, then, standing back
against a wall, waiting for you, woman new

with the baby on your arms. Oh, the weight
the waiting feel in their jaws, biting just hard
enough to keep from bleeding. Here, let me

say it simply: there was a small & silly girl
there the morning he was born, & once
he was she wasn't. She took to sleeping

in the woodshed, in the shadowed branches,
in the hum of hornets gutting green apples,
& sometimes I could hear her hammering

C to D minor (quietly, so as not to wake him).
Chin to the windowsill, keeping rhythm with rain,
waiting for the bird that chose us both to swim

to surface   our water   frozen   halves
        a white & narrow road   he enters
                her   your world   cold of laughter.

Small Break in the Cirrocumulus

Backlit in a night sky, dangerously
     ordinary   almond or eye

     or almond-shaped eye
in my right breast. *Fibroadenoma*. Or

I only get to breathe for so long.
     Tell me I'm dying already,

     so I can pick up my life
& move it. There was a woman there,

in that cancer institute (a mountain
     among mountains but glass

     above a city in a dry lakebed),
pushing a cart of juice & granola

& knit caps for people who consider that
     place a second home.

     It was another planet.
Everyone knew something I didn't.

I almost cried riding the elevator up
     & riding down, I cupped my hand

     under my breast, held nothing more
than the world.   I smell grass & horses

     & bacon.   All I'll ever be.

To Sleep

not as a woman who brews tea & kneels
on rice but one who swims with narcolepsy,

who cinches all the alleys into darkness
& fells trees, who forces a bit into the mouth

of aurora borealis until the moon parades
its wounds in color, until her limbs go numb

scene by scene, by sleight of hand, by flip
turning in a lukewarm pool between what walls

we build, between what shocks we tuck in
tight, between what we somersault & dredge

from our eyes at the temperature of sleep
without drowning, without burning

our temples, without righting the lies we tell
our minds to make us fade, to make us stay

still & take it, to make us love paralysis
to such a point we jump in water, legless.

View from the High Road

It is as you'd expect beyond the rusting guardrails
      tacked to gravel s-curves & switchbacks:

a maze of sandstone fins & cactus beds, tumbleweed
      clogging all the yucca shoots. There is no sky

because you're already in it, high on that high road
      where the air thins out to shallow gasps

& your mule refuses to carry anything. Your feet
      are one steep grade from gangrene, & even

though you know the scene is the stuff of a movie,
      you won't shove a mule just to watch

a prop swallow the view. If not for this road,
      nothing. Quicksand. A coffee can of pecans

you'll send back after he leaves in the night.
      Some black sky with its sharp, sharp moon,

& you with your neck stretched like shadow.
      In the distance of those fins, he is

forever bending, collecting those hard-shell nuts
      he knows you can't eat. Your throat swells

with the thought of him four states gone,
      his boots resoled & restitched. But fuck it.

So you were a stop on the way to somewhere
       else. Spring for priority shipping, jerk

the dustcover down behind you. Trot cleanly away.

My Desert

My desert has many steeples & prays
        to no one. A fence at the flames
            of sagebrush & tumbleweed,

my desert sleeps bootheels to assbones.
        She dreams in petroglyph panels.
            When my desert travels, she steers

by the compass of a rattlesnake's tongue.
        She skins prairie dogs with a butterfly
            knife. My desert needs no canteen,

no poncho, no saddle or horse. Give her moon
        shine, filterless tobacco, the biggest belt
            buckle west of the Great Divide.

My desert believes in the power of a fault line,
        that every grain of sand will map its way
            back to an ocean. She knows

busted spines & rummaged potsherds & sun-
        rusted aluminum cans. By night, she has
            summoned her widows to ruin

sites & shawled & thorned & ribbed her cacti.
        She's scrawled survival on the vulture's bones
            & wrung one last drop for the juniper

root, pluming through rock. My desert pretends
        she's not a desert at all: her cracked bowl,
            her impassable walls, her lake poisoned

by salt. But my desert knows what waterless means.
        Some nights, she walks bootless into the cold
                & strikes a match just to grow

warm again. All winter long, my desert
        cups her hand to her ear, she kneels, she listens
                to those ragged peaks, where all is come

& all is lost & all is searching for the moment
        when my desert will make lakes again
                from snow, & we'll lie down & float.

Barefoot on the Pulpit

Backstage, we don't kiss for an empty auditorium. We kiss

for strangers who meet & unmeet, the way cobble paths

halt just short of stained glass. Who knows why I won't

let you know me on the porch swing. A flat beer. A story

of a woman confused then dead now gone from you. Now.

Don't speak of what I have in a home so many miles away.

Let's leave this at campus cats & sewer raccoons, that herd

of deer crossing against the traffic signal that never flashes

yellow or red. Here, it's not the stopping that worries us.

We're breaking into buildings when we should be sleeping,

scaling fire escapes toward every crenellated ledge,

& when I barefoot up the stairs that wind to the pulpit,

where a whole organ of faces fills an empty church, you ask

how it feels to be there, so much gold, so much breath.

For My First Dog

I've rehearsed my whimper, tattered
the tissue & balled it in my pocket
so when I say that *it just didn't work*
& they take you back to a cage,
the volunteers will think I've cried,

that I'll keep on crying. But you're a dog,
learning a hot stove with your whole face.
You don't expect me to defrost the rear
window, to lie. I'll say you chased my cat
until she slept & ate on a closet shelf,

that you broke the crate & barked all day
at my nylons draped over the shower rod
because it's true. Because you wouldn't stop
worrying the wound for which there was no
tourniquet, licking each suture to infection.

Because it's easy to confuse hurt with clean
when nothing cinches a hollow but skin. *No*

the vet will say—that I'm projecting
onto a spayed dog—but who, if not
a woman, would chew through her flesh
& die with the taste of an empty cradle
in her mouth? Of course I've gone too far.

I slipped a cone over your head & felt my hands
wash the blood from my mother's hair,
rouge the yellow from her high cheekbones
which are my cheekbones, though the eyes
are mine alone & green.

Notes

"After the Fire": The phrase "hears his dead dog / breathing, & he won't touch imaginary things" is appropriated from "I Am Poem," written by my son Channer Krause in 2008.

"My Lake": After Sandra Beasley.

"The Lapidary Speaks": The phrase "there is no death" in the imagined epigraph is a reference to Walt Whitman's "Song of Myself."

"Errata": After Yusef Komunyakaa.

"Family Portrait as the Language of Disaster": Some terms and concepts are borrowed from the Federal Emergency Management Agency's Natural Disaster RMS Publications, which can be found at https://www.fema.gov/what-mitigation/security-risk-management-series-publications#1.

"Love & Squall": Inspired by Andrew Wyeth's painting *Squall*.